pain
as
penance

Ravyn Wells

PAGE PUBLISHING
Conneaut Lake, PA

First originally published by Page Publishing 2024

ISBN 979-8-89157-376-5 (pbk)
ISBN 979-8-89157-393-2 (digital)

Printed in the United States of America

To Lily, my childhood dog
To Aunt Louise and bacon pancakes
To Dr. Roxi and therapy wins!
To my family and friends, for your support
To Rachael because we made it

ACT ONE

Swimming in Stars

Blindness

stars blink awake
        spearing through the cosmos night after night.
tonight their light lands
        near my weary walker, restless as the night stretches.
burning, knowing that the entire
        universe walks with you.

Relative to a Star

we are finite.
we are a blot on a blank page delirious from rebirth.

we are staccato rain music weaving bright tomorrows.
we are homesick for places that don't remember us.

we are the final heavy step from a cliff's edge, waiting for wings.

Beauties and Beasts

Break off petals, leave the center
      bare to the wind.

Curtain it away, seclude the
      freakish beauty.

Cut off their noses and
      declare myself God.

Somehow find beauty in bared skin
      bared thoughts.

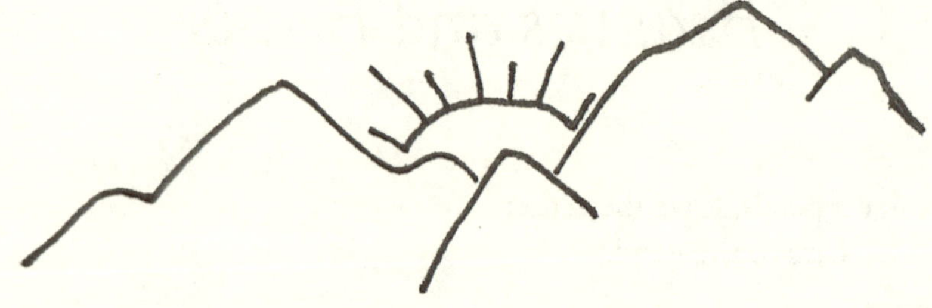

Wildest Dreams

Testament to time and earth, I scale

A mountain
Its strong winds cut through gloves and punish those who dare climb.

Then the summit

A world stretched out in front of me as one of the heavens
As the gentle sun opens my eyes and I freeze

And I whisper

I am here.

Easter Day

I prayed for a stranger today
        panic and fear staining its edges yellow.
I held my hope tightly in my palm
        reluctant to release it
As my fingers curled open
        it flitted out and leapt into a sky so blue my eyes ached.

Crying if he could not,
crying out for someone to protect him. To keep him safe.
To hold his hand, reminding him to live.

I have only seen his face once
yet I understand.

Understanding

No god will
      gift
you a pamphlet on divinity

but if I do not know myself
      how
do I expect others to?

Act Two

A Terrible Deep Silence

Escape

Asleep in my memories
my eyes ignore a different timeline
behind blue eyes.

In a stolen moment,
I did not believe in God
or a Father.

Green eyes hover over mine;
don't blink.

Stare down a future clouded with
uncertainty and believe in
myself.

Oblivion

Do you know what oblivion tastes like,
friend?

For I know its delicate fizz as a silky promise.
Gentle rocking to the melody and ignore the danger in the water.
A midnight murmur, raw joy, flowing from sore eyes.

It tastes of freedom and flight,
I could fly if only given wings,
I could soar if given glue and feathers,
I could jump if only given a ledge.

It tastes of summer rain, rolling
deep tremors in the bones of trees
demanding the world to wake.

It does not question,
does not judge the direction of the river.

It is the handrail on the tower,
the rope on the boat,
the harness on a cliff,
a promise of more tomorrow.

Addiction trails a whisper of
nothingness past my eyes
that I can't help but
chase into the dark.

I Need a Break

bitter flavors dissolve
      across my tongue with a
sweet aftertaste.

pink velvet skies
      should be enough for
my eyes, my soul.

still wishing for my mind
      to escape with me
faster than before.

Escapism

Chasing daydreams, I wander through
endless storylines, pick and choose
heroes, villains.

Blink away holograms of what could
be what could be what
could be.

Outpace light itself on a mission to find a reality where I fit.

Fashion thousands of lives, loves, and losses in memory only.

I warp reality to feign strength and embellish
life in glass rubies, emeralds, and pearls.

Shatter them when I grow bored.

Forge a new story with the glittering remains.

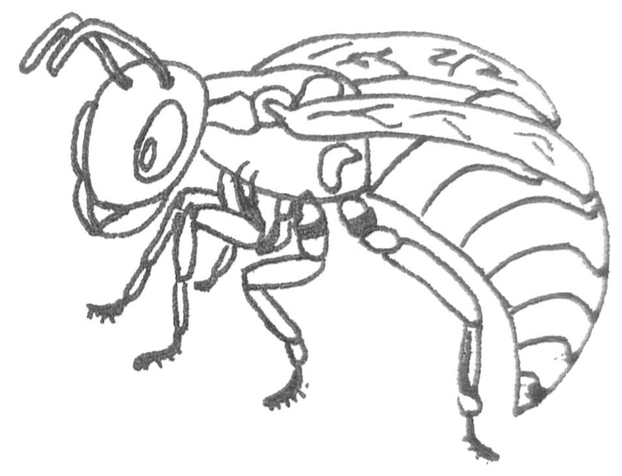

Reflection

Skin is littered with disgust
      sown by a different hand.

Eyes are sore from barricading
      enough tears to drown the world in.

Mouth is full of wet, rotten soil
      watered till roots flood.

Head is trapped with wasps engaged in
      scorched earth warfare.

"*Just George*"

I feel the center of my being splinter and spin around a star of glass.

Control over my mind is flimsy at best
steel at worst.
What can one offer besides
inconsistency between bouts of life?
      Seas of dread sink our dreams.

Thoughts and memories and self-scattered at best
at worst incomplete.

Ignorant

Demand proof of reality without
using your eyes.

Ignore the validity of your existence.

Remove your opinion in
search for the void.

Leaping from oblivion to
Oblivion to avoid confronting the truth.

To want an oblivion so sweet everything
after is sour.

Oblivion is the reality of fools
yet, here I cling.

Awake

Met at crossroads of fear
       and loss—
consequence screams toward me.

Met at crossroads of clarity
       and belonging—
I am the consequence.

Long Car Ride

Always fractured but
somehow this moment is different.

Breaking quietly in
      the backseat of my life.

Hoping someone will see,
turn around,
offer a hand.

To stop asking

why are you so loud

why are you so much

My hands remove me from reality,
erase the sounds of the oblivious.

Lonely

Recurring daydreams with scripted conversations
convince yourself someone is there
      hugging mirrors

Suffocate in the vise of empty car seats

Wind down familiar paths to dig
      deeper into darkness
I have crawled this path before
      recognize worms and roots

How have I lost myself again?

Escapism

Once, when I wasn't mine,
       I blinded eyes to escape.

I turned mirrors inside out,
       music outside in.

I belonged to the dark interior
       of the underside of beds.

I slept in the wools and nylons
       surrounded by sneakers.

Built walls made of others words
       and worlds, protected—safe.

Hunger

I am exhausted of constant hunger.

Nothing satiates the groans, echoing states of disarray, organs knotted.

How to explain:

Rumbling of acid, demanding more
for more than I can consume.

Crushing of a not-strong-enough mind, demanding more
for more than this life could offer.

Sensitive pale skin, demanding more
for more warmth, for less winter.

I am hunger: I am razors devouring emotion
diminish them until they are wisps of flavor.

I am starved for a moment when I am not hungry.

ACT THREE

Sitting with Loneliness

Blank Canvas

Is it not odd to see a painting move?

Illusions of color blind the curious eye but are fixed

They grow closer yet stay
behind thick red ropes intend to separate

Wonder if I can be as great
without losing myself

Wonder if I am following
the same path of destruction.

A Bit Egotistical,
Don't You Think?

Is it an overinflated ego saying, I relate to the Greats
        of paint, and music, and word
Yet I see myself in four cut sunflowers.

I am finding myself at a loss
        of experience in emotion
While being constantly overwhelmed by them.

How dare I compare my
        journey to that of great people
Far more accomplished at my age.

Compare the purple inks of
        suffering, misery
To feel less alone.

To become the Sunflower Emperor—we
        sacrifice our souls
to progress, to art, to perfection

while I chip away at china.

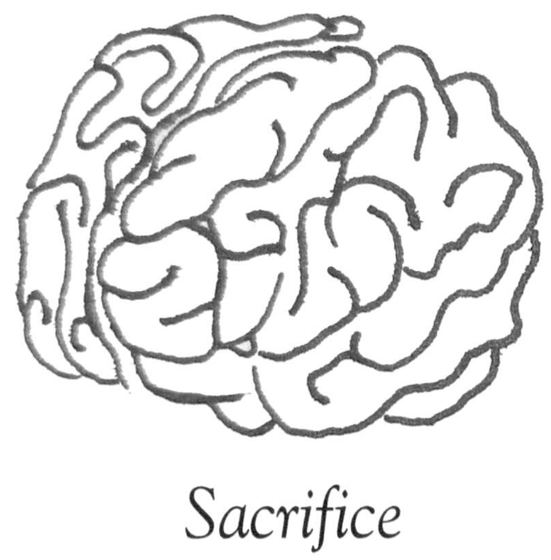

Sacrifice

I may yet lose the ability to create works of the soul
to preserve my mind.

Burn brightly as Mercury chasing the Sun
melt my atmosphere and char landscapes
all so I can burn
in a sky full of brighter stars.

Fight for my place among named
spots of light.

Fight through days encased in ice
with others ending in flames.

"Hope Is a Thing with Feathers"

Hope is not friendly.

I grit my teeth when it appears,
shoulders carry heavier loads.

I do not invite Hope.
The promise of new beginnings,
of fathers accepting their children.

Give them another chance, be
patient, be gentle,
be accommodating.

I ask rhetorically, bitter from a refusal of a future.

I avoid eye contact with Hope.

So often feathers of brilliance
disguise the fiery trail behind it.

Shoot down the thing with feathers
pluck it, sell a mirage of tomorrows.

"Dickinson"

Death came for me in the
hours of in-between.
In their chariots for pharaohs,
they visit the graves of the forgotten.

Death lost me in the
slipping of fingers, "Not your time."
In my search for oblivion, I
visit Death at their throne.

Death does not want me
full of promises for next time.

Praying for this to be the next
time, but that I stay with Death.
I plead for a chance to be rid
of the emotions of humanity.

Clawing at my skin, my mind
brings no glance of pity.

They have seen worse, they
know I am not at the breaking point.
Death is waiting for me,
but I do not want to wait for Death.

Act Four

Medicines and Migraines

Reality Check

Diagnose me,
give me the damage I haven't caused yet.

Tell me the mistakes I will create,
give me the path I take.

Something lost in translation

Give me something I can change,
I am lost in the pills of a fixed reality.

I am told I cannot change my mind—
chemicals lie to me as I lie to them.

"Forget" to take reality management
experiment with my own madness.

Slipping into comfy sweats,
the same hoodie, same socks.

Don't shower—repulsed by my existence
dirt piles under jagged nails.

Waking up, expected the same, fully
confronted with a wave of Righteousness.

Reality Cashed

Scream as the volume thuds car windows because we can.
Spend money because we have it.

Obsession fuels the sleepless nights and
threaten a fallout, a collapse of fragile construct.

Sunrise of realizing, I am nothing if not broken.

Side Effects

Stumble from kitchen to couch
eyes of concrete.

Hands, knees, toes, asleep
before my mind is.

Dizziness sets in last, rising from the fort of pillows.

Too much time wasted on
regulating pills that
regulate me.

Choke

6:50 a.m.

Drink.
Tilt head back.
Drop pills to back of throat.
Choke.
Swallow.
Drink again.

9:30 p.m.

Drink (× 3)
Tilt head.
Drop pills.
Choke.
They refuse to go down.
Go to sink.
Ribs, throat squeezing.

Try again.

Drop pills.
Choke.
Swallow.
Drink again.

Off

Vivid symphony of colors
    feeling the clashes and bursts.
Breathing deeply of acrid air
    yet satisfied with each inhale.
Mind untethered and skittish
    dart from one thought to the next.
Time slows and warps
    Dali would be proud.

On

Organize emotions into their own boxes
    labeled and sorted.
Short breaths, only take what the body needs
    heavily regulated.
Slow, steady marching of minds
    no room for impulse.
Time behaves and doesn't wander
    yet I struggle.

Level 8 Migraine

My eyes fill with sand as a hammer pounds home a steady cadence
ripple of sound follows a flood of pain.

Immobile and blind I creep toward anywhere
anywhere on my knees, bruising hands.

Tiptoe through a minefield and brace for impact.

Intracranial Hypertension Symptom

my eyes never truly close
even if my eyelashes brush my cheeks, oil spills
explode across the depths of an ocean. My
unconscious mind? My soul?

questions of "what are you" reflect back to me as the white
violet light pulses through me.
my eyes are open even as they are shut.

Sunrise Sunset

darkened skies give way to ambers, lavenders, cherries, and roses.
a day passes with a whimper
so it begins with a bang and grumbles about bright light and burnt
 coffee.

silent rooms give way to noise, shouting, and demanding attention.
a day passes with a bang
so it ends with a whimper and hiding beneath blankets nursing an
 ice pack.

Sudden Migraines

Add another page in the book
flip through with
a listless eye—sharpen.

Raging waters rush into cracks of my skull
condemn my mind unlivable.

Pray to any gods that will listen—
      for eyes not screaming
      for minds not on fire.

The flood ends as quickly as it began—
      deep breaths
flip another page.

Be Careful What You Wish For

To think I wished for pain, to
end numb nerves.

Now my plea is for numbness, to
quell waves of pain.

My solace, intoxicating melody, now
ruins my eyes.

Another wave erupts, creeping up
behind my tears.

Being crushed under my own command
add more weight.

Migraines

Drilling for oil and finding
exact spots in my skull where pain seeps
and dig
into gray, red, white matter.

Black rot covers my hands
slick and reflecting the terror on my face
and scream
demand retribution.

Imposter Syndrome

I don't know if I am
faking
all my flaws
but I find myself

Waking—frantic, heavy
not enough air.

I can taste panic; not mine, theirs.

Eyes stare
pain and fear lit my body,
shaking adrenaline off.

I don't belong.

The Comfort of Pain

Ah, Despair, dear friend, I thought
you had lost your way back
to my veins, my breath.

Where had you gone, amid the
lyrical hope, warmth and
satin sunsets? Where had you?

Your footprints run the trenches
that dig alongside my arms
length; deep, caressing.

Ah, Despair, dear friend, I had
forgotten the sour taste you left
in my veins, my breath.

Helpless

Cement blocks conceal my hands
     feet dangle above a fast nothing
frozen seeping into my bones.

Beg for someone to save me
free me from sin.

Sunlight ebbs from eyes as it whispers my name
     pushes farther, deeper

Reach for the orange that's not there while I fade
from view, helpless.

Sometimes I Still Want to Hurt Me

serrate my bones
chip away imperfections
prepare for a future of lying still.

bathtubs and rivers running red
limp hair and arms
crave the ache
so sweet
so precise
depraved.

inspect my existence in millimeters
salt in invisible wounds.

Stairway of Heaven

what waits
for me at the bottom of ledges?
how do I climb without
stairs made of pills? I no longer
care when I slam into rock bottom. Embrace bones
breaking to feel anything
besides fog. Who would love
me without medication that erases
ledges and mountains? Obstacles
spring forward when I am alone so
look into my eyes and
convince me I'm not broken. That
something doesn't need to be
mended—fences trampled by
sheep I lost count of. Look at my face
tell me I'm not flawed—tell me I am more than
ghosts of regret.

ACT FIVE

Desire and Regret Are Twins

Strongest Regret

In another reality,
        could I have been yours?

The sweetest regret I taste when I remember
        green eyes, gentle with
        what could have been.

What would you think like?
What would you feel like?

Plagued by the impossibility of us.

Stolen

I want you to cling to me
      as I am oxygen
      and you are adrift
      lost in space
      as I am without you.

The piano guides our
      feet, spinning into
      our perfectly
      imagined
      future.

To never share a home
      without knowing
      who we were
      fill it with
      bitter scents of
      regret.

Spike

Sacrifice everything for someone
       blind to my devotion.

Countless times to prove
       I am the kind of man that
       deserves your attention.

Determine that I am not
       the kind of person to
       smile without pain.

Yet I am still a kind of person
       worthy.

A Poem That Rhymes

I am full of contradiction
With none so much as a bent
Rotten nail infected with spite

Bringing forth a fruition
Only I've dreamt
Painting in lavender white

Beautiful Noise

Laughter, surprising to be heard,
shoots from my smile
and he says it is beautiful.

We shout songs about birds,
about love, heartache, and bliss
and he says it is beautiful.

Moans, escaping pillows
whispering forever and promises
and he says it is beautiful.

My eyes shed the anger, the loss
desperate, lost confused—how did this happen
and he says it is beautiful.

Moment B

Blank staring at eyes
Unflinching.
Lecture and ramble as ears
Ignore.
Hope shriveled as disgust takes
Root.
Yellow walls, leech gray, and high school
Returns.
Wonder where the fantasy
Ended.

Moment A

I have found a
soul
among the clouds.

Pastel watercolors dilute across the lazy sky.

Their hues deepen,
mimicking
the intricacies of life.

She floats
along a loaded edge, a hand
pointed to the heavens
a hand pointed to below.

A delicate bud preening
in the sunlight—
Who dares
to create her shadow?

A Lust for Life

A desire to see stars, gritting their teeth against space like me
long to taste salt and honeysuckle and lips
My body yearns for your arms wrapping around my pieces
hold me together.

Eyes burn with flames that light a lust for life.

Flirt

I am for the chase.
The elevated heart rates and a flush creeping
on your cheekbones while I move in time to your breathing.

The teasing, promises of more hidden behind clear eyes.

Back and forth we pull and dance and weave between ourselves.

Abandon indecision to make the first move.

Moonlight

To see the light
      dripping from her fingers,
      whipping in circles
      arms spread dancing.

Joy and freedom guide
      sure feet in the duet of eyes
      locking
      matching energies;
      the frequency of life.

She entertains reality
      teases an audience
      haunted by her legs,
      her hair, her lips.

Nothing falling to ground
      but my knees, begging a
      sullen child to forgive,
      to take her hand.

Strawberry Girl

I met my strawberry girl today
     in separate gardens we were sown.
Different parts of the picnic
     I can't stop the ants picking away.
I crave blue skies and
     saccharine memories
     burnt peaches and sunflower seeds.

I lost my strawberry girl to
     escape the garden walls.
Reaching a hand to freedom
     fingers covered in nettles.

My Body

Lemon fingertips sweeping open
    eyes, breaking
    barriers of breath.

Caress the newness, exquisite.
    Noting every dip and bend,
    all the cracks and divots.

Lost in a foreign landscape, guide
    my hands
    create a map with blazing skin.

The Future Her

Eyes of a goddess, exploring
into love and devotion.

Gasoline lips burn my skin
craving more—faster.

Cigarettes and shoulders
brush the ash from my eye.

Imagination

The pink satin flits across
tongues, sinking into ice veins.

Delicate movements with
all intentions laid bare.

All of anything I hold back,
unleashed onto my hesitation.

T

Aphrodite draped like
careless things.

Whispers of together, of
a place to shield from twin mothers.

A silken southern drawl, wrapping its
arms in the warm air.

Bathing in the simple praise
of belonging.

Act Six

Blood in the Water

How Can I Help?

Bitter words leak from eyes like mine—
his eyes.

Reach out a hand, a hope—
but how?

I don't know what I can do
about the rage that thrives in him
without getting hurt.

But I cannot leave
him alone
with his bitter thoughts.

True Terror

Waiting for the dark blow
      praying for the end.

Frantic eyes while breath
      flinches at every hand.

Terrified of his loneliness
      more to be alone with him.

I wish for his mind to forgive
      not at the cost of my mind.

Brother Mine

I see myself in his image
      a hurt child asking anyone to care
      yet hurting those who are too close
      to the truth.

Reach a hand into the flames again
Knowing the burn will come
      yet hoping it will be gentler this time.

Brothers

Brothers are the umbrella in a storm
or
The ones throwing the snowballs.

Older—Protective. Classic.
    Ring leader as a shining city on a hill.
    First to smile, last
    to cast a tired glance.

Younger—Adventures. Mischief.
    Instigator with a cocky Cheshire grin.
    Head first into trouble, last
    to name others.

Constant Comparison

Be more like your brother
Be more like your sister
Be anyone but you.

Mold my clay into an image of yourself
and treat me as a toy.

I am your creation yet you do not
handle with care
rather feed me backhanded compliments.

Fed up, my throat closes, words seething
to finally release.

Skin of platinum and diamond
pressurized with rage.

Smothered into a perfect bowl
porcelain doll.

Ivory, clean but not
polished, worn and cracked.

Feign surprise after years of perfectly
placed barbs splinter glass bones.

Recurring Nightmare

My name at the time
        whispered
from my left,
as Mom.

Three more once-my-names
        erupt
to my right,
as Dad.

More dart from tall grass to nip at exposed skin
        calling
        cursing
        shouting
for attention, I turn away.

Time drags its feet as my mind fill of
        screaming
chants of No Mercy
all disguised as names.

Retreat to stainless steel walls
        panic
cover hearts with insulation
crawl through glass to safety.

Mother, May I?

Becoming one's mother is not
one fell swoop.

Excessive acts of a parent
consumed
by their own rattlesnake thoughts.

A quiet evaluation of my reflection
proves a hypothesis.

I have become her
      in the way I fear
      the most.

Broken arms can't pull my weight off concrete.

Legs can't outrun what waits in my blood, my mind.

Exhausted with a core of fragile egos.

I'm Not Scared of the Dark

Feral fears create themselves in
darkness
Creating limbs, digits, teeth
Rotten flesh and a core
of unknown origins

Even this ghastly image
pales
and shrinks back

The one person that is meant to protect from the dark—
"I wish you were born different"

Sometimes I wish that too

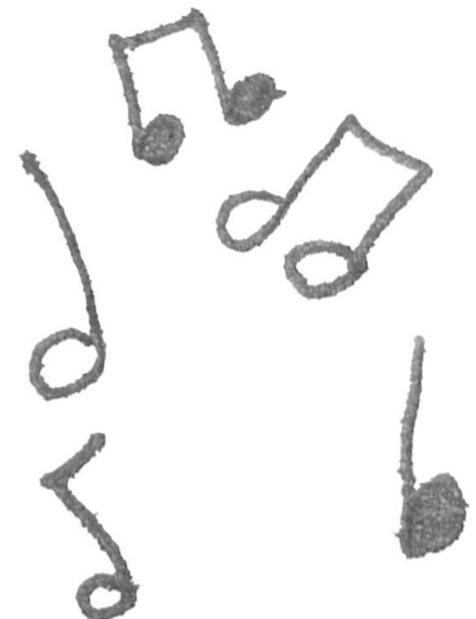

Mom Used to Croon

The crooked grin of mischief beckons me to the kitchen,
fingers curled around the music spinning through the room.

Passing by blurs of laughter, burst pink and yellow, our hands
mingling with matching hair and footwork.

We could never speak to each other, only
listen to music with knotted souls.

Brown Oxfords

I wore these shoes as I walked
across a sunlit stage.

Mixed emotions roaring in my ears, I almost
missed them calling my name.

Shake hands and smile because I did it
and I'm proud.

I scan the crowd, searching for family
that wasn't coming.

The smile glitches and I fight
to keep it on as another shutter clicks.

My throat closes tighter than my grip
on a faux leather book.

but

A bottom lip trembles,
fears spill over and I silently weep for my tired heart.

Distance and Fondness

I realized today, I had forgotten what my Dad sounds like.
Mom's tone.

The revelation caused my feet to pause, stumble.
Another pearl of truth.

The audience of reprimands, judgment before the day comes.
Had been dormant.

I am not ignorant.

I know someday the accusing screams will make its weight known again.
Today, I celebrate that I have allowed myself to forget.

When the World Was Beautiful

Blossoms of summer days
spent as a
wild thing

Travel up my arms
once more

Find the wonder of a child
a believer
of everything this world can be

It is difficult to remember a time
with smooth skin and wrinkled shirts

I have become the opposite of my child.

Healing a Child

Eating ice cream for dinner
and cake for lunch.
Talking in voices that aren't really me to
giggle and laugh about little things.

Say it out loud, everything
you forgot
and not be judged, loathed, or shamed.

To let the birds fly from beneath my skin
Fly me to tomorrow.

Daydreams

Grass tickles my ears and spiders play
in my shoes while I find bears and ducks,
dragons, and mermaids disguised in wispy clouds lazily
drifting across a sky too big for me to hold.

A sneeze creeps into my nose and when it
erupts, tufts of dandelions take flight with blue jays mocking
chastising for breaking the silence.

Moments when nothing was
happening and everything was preparing to breathe
in deep mouthfuls of soggy air punctuated by clover pollen.

Days of perfect abandon when no one called my name and I
    disappeared.

Reborn as the nefarious captain of the mightiest pirate ship to ever
    trawl these waters.
A swordsman, defending my land and people, with any sword I could
    find. A king
running from an usurper, betrayed by love,
fighting bandits and knights with stolen honor.

Bare feet follow the paths only
deer know, navigate fallen limbs and dastardly evil plots.
Shouts of bravery, victory, and cries of vengeance, spilled blood.

Summers when I read books of kings and
thieves, sailors, and pirates, desperately cling
to warm skin and summer rain while cursing
biting mosquitoes and a dull reality.

Boy in the Italian Restaurant

Color my skies with blues from eyes.

Let the green of theirs slowly grow
meet me in a tomorrow.

Where we are both
stronger than our fears, our
parents have no hold.

Reach hands out to lead our
tomorrow.

Aunt Louise

Found love
        warmth and peace
a complete love
requiring nothing but to hear and be heard.

Safety in measures of cinnamon, eggs, and bread
dashes of sugar.

I do not know how else to name this
but
love.

Bucket List

Doing everything I have never had the
        courage
to try before

Find peace in warm salt water, up too
        late
drink too much

Smile so hard I forget I've ever felt fear.

Act Seven

Identity Crisis (Plural)

It's Meant to Challenge You

My battle should have been
"how do I make friends"

My challenge should have been
"what to wear to school"

My fear should have been
"what do I want to be"

Not

"I don't want to be"

Insecurity

Ugly thoughts drip down cheeks
tense from restraint.

Boiling away—down to
an augmented reality.

Peel away feverish eyes
then the stretched skin.

"Not enough" marches a path
down my nose, carving
their tremors into my knees.

My Broken Name

Why is the mirror lying to me?

Why do my ears cry false names?

I have owned this name—
it has traveled across time with me.

But why does it not recognize me?

Let me hear and not blink
twice, to remember, oh. Me.

To say it and not feel a twinge
phantom limb pain of past mistakes.

Excuses, Excuses

Irritation rears a mottled green head
Continue to demand for respect deserved

Determine what lines to draw while they use
That is not. My. Name.

Impossibility as an excuse.

Declare War on She

They lay in a bed of roses
      pruned and promising.
Soft against my cheek, the
      scent, quiet and still.

She rips the thorns and sends
      pinpricks into my nerves.
Painting the roses red so every
      flinch, an internal correction.

Intentional or ignorant, she
      itches between my toes.
Persistent flares evolve into
      flames, roaring agony.

The courage to speak has never been farther from me.

Rachael

Remind me, little one,
what did you wish for?
Once, upon a star, hoping
for everything you deserved.

Light the small candle and
find a midnight moon answering.

How to Make a New Name

I want my name to hurtle
through the stars.
To burn as bright wishes
thrown into the cosmos.

I want my name to grow
and flower the ground beneath.
To bloom in a forest of
futures, and creatures.

I want my name to be a
scream ripping through time.
To be the reason planets come
into being and stars explode.

I want my name to mean more
than syllables to get my attention.
To be muttered or shouted, letters
I don't relate to anymore.

I want *my* name to be a
ripple in water, creating chaos.
Chaos that implodes what others
see me as—so they see *me*.

I want my own name.

A name I can say out loud and recognize in the mirror.

A name to go with a face
my parents made
and my eyes stole.

"This Is Me"

A voice raises to the beams
adorned with cobwebs and forgotten ornaments.

Music stomps dust from windows
birds from roosts
feet from concrete.

A crowd of empty applause
swarms, hands stretch for a rose.

Crescendo of muscles, begging
to float again.

ACT EIGHT

Grief and Why I Can't Hold Her

Tears

Tears hold a certainty of time.
They are the minute hand to
determine schedules to fit grief.

Sagging shoulders betray the
concealed sleepless nights.

They are the stitches that
overlap and fold time.

Hesitant beginnings, that
close eyes, ears, mouths.
They are the aches of a once blaze,
bitter with lemon and salt.

Begging for the intimacy
of speaking alone, low and sure.
They are the desperate, black lightning
pooling obsidian.

They are the final breath wasted,
cool eyes and steady voices.

"*Heart-stopper*"

Jealousy, bittersweet
runs a swift course through me.

Chase it with longing
    for a different past
    different parents.
Not so different but not what was mine.

Seeing mothers
    fathers
embrace their children
    with confusion, yes
but with more love.

To realize it is not my fault
    and to believe it.

Even now, grown and growing, I find
    after years of searching for a me
I was never able to find,
    they still react with anger,
    barbs of trust.

Tears collected and leapt from swollen, aching eyes.
I grieved for time lost
    to fog mixed with reality.

I grieved for the child that did not see themselves
    in the mirror, but a stranger.

I wept for what I had lost then and
    what I am losing now.

There Are Days

confidence and bravery
wearing what I want and feeling
safe in my skin.

I belong in this place
but
there are days when I can't breath
days that pass me in blinks,
barely remember what it feels like to
fit in my body.

there are days when clocks melt
time dripping by and I am trapped again.

my hands are full of holes
full of lost time.

I Have Trouble Crying

I have to paint my face
on my canvas and be satisfied with
results.

I need a mirror, the reverse of me to
capture the rough skin and lonely
eyes.

Eyes that only cry when someone else's pain distracts me.

Eyes that only cry when I am alone.

Who Is Grief?

Everyone says loss is like a hole
        a chasm aching to be filled.

They are uncomfortable with an absence
            waiting, counting the ticking of clocks.

I do not feel a hole or a void
yet constantly empty.

Am I the hole?

Lily at 18

I forget from time to time
      what my grief feels like

I can function day to day without losing
      myself to painful memories

Then reminders of innocence and
      unrelenting love trickle in

My grief knocks and slowly enters
      this time

Grief holds me as she whispers
      loss and heartache into my tears

Once a destructive lover, Grief
      comforts my torn heart
      with no judgments.

Epitaph for Rachael

Bones do not rest here and memories need not die.
In a quiet cedar coffin there are rather shadows.
A child poured in silicon molds that did not cure.
Modeling clay worked too long.
Begging for someone to listen, desperate for love.

A child brave enough to make sacrifices to keep me safe.

Let her rest.

About the Author

Ravyn Wells is a first-time author from South Carolina. Born in 1999, they grew up spending their time in the woods and at soccer practice, always with a book in hand. Creative by nature, Ravyn is a painter and loves to draw as well.

As the second oldest of four, high school was spent at soccer, football, and wrestling matches and also at church every Sunday with family. Ravyn tutored others in high school, which led to a love for teaching and a desire to help others learn and love the classroom. They currently live in Arizona as an Earth and Space Science teacher with fifteen very loved plants and an overwhelming love of the stars.

www.ingramcontent.com/pod-product-compliance
Lightning Source LLC
Chambersburg PA
CBHW022027150726
47990CB00002B/842